D1825221

PROFILES

QueenVictoria

Lesley Young

Illustrated by
Gordon King

Evans Brothers Limited

Published by Evans Brothers Limited
2A Portman Mansions
Chiltern Street
London W1M 1LE

First published in Great Britain in 1980 by
Hamish Hamilton Children's Books

Reprinted 1984, 1987, 1992 (twice)

Typeset by Pioneer
Printed by Stephens & George Ltd,
    South Wales, Great Britain.
       Tel: 0685 5351

ISBN 0 237 60001 3

Titles in this series

Contents

1 When She Was Good

In April, 1819, a large shabby coach rattled into Dover. It was packed with trunks, pets, a bedstead, servants, a doctor and midwife — and a very pregnant Duchess of Kent. The coach had been driven all the way from Germany by the Duke of Kent himself. He had been told by a gypsy that he would have a daughter who would be a great queen, and he was determined that his child should be born in England.

May 24th, 1819, was a typical English spring day — chilly with light rain. In the early hours of the morning the Duchess of Kent gave birth to a healthy girl — 'as plump as a partridge'. She was christened Alexandrina Victoria — and was known as Drina for short. The Duke, who was the fourth son of King George III, was overjoyed. His child was, he exclaimed, 'truly a model of strength and beauty combined!' Like any new father, his thoughts ran ahead to the pleasures he would share with his daughter: riding, holidays by the sea, picture-books in the nursery.

But little Drina never knew her father. When she was only eight months old, he caught a cold, which soon became a chill. His illness was not helped by his doctors, who 'bled' him, using leeches and other devices. He lost

over six pints of blood, and not surprisingly died soon afterwards. So little Drina grew up in the shadow of her father's memory.

A week after her father's death, Drina's grandfather, King George III, also died and his eldest son, the 58-year-old Prince Regent, became George IV. As soon as she could talk, George IV was 'Uncle King' to Drina. The King was amused by his small niece with the big blue eyes, whose life as an only child among adults had given her an assurance beyond her years. Drina was not at all frightened by his fat, gouty figure, topped by an elaborate wig — or by the way that he growled 'give us your little paw' at her, when he wished her to shake the royal hand. She was, however, taken aback when he kissed her. She found that his face was covered with thick, greasy make-up to hide the bags and wrinkles. But even at such an early age, Drina was more interested in personality than appearance, and she was very fond of her uncle.

On one of Drina's visits to Windsor, there was a concert in the conservatory. 'What is your favourite tune?' asked the King. 'God Save the King,' she replied at once, and he ordered the band to play it for her. The King was so delighted he presented her with a miniature of himself set in diamonds. In place of a father, Drina turned for advice to one of her mother's brothers, Leopold. Although he later became King Leopold I of Belgium, he lived in England during Drina's childhood. She came to rely on him and, throughout her life, asked his opinion on complicated matters of state.

But by far the greatest influence on Drina's childhood was her German governess, Louise Lehzen — always 'dear Lehzen' to Drina. It was her job to supervise Drina's behaviour as well as her lessons. Languages came easily to the child: she spoke fluent French and German and fairly good Italian. Most of all she enjoyed her art lessons. The sketches and watercolours which she did in the nursery were the first of hundreds that she produced during her long life. Lessons in deportment were not such fun. Sometimes a bunch of prickly holly was pinned beneath her chin to help her to remember to hold her head high as she walked about the Palace. The stately bearing she learned in this way stood her in good stead, for she only just topped 1.5 metres. 'Everyone grows but me!' she once said in disgust.

Although Drina enjoyed music, she preferred

listening rather than trying to play herself with her fat little fingers. When her piano teacher told her there was no royal road to music, and that she must practise like everyone else, Drina crossly slammed the lid of the piano shut and said 'There! There is no must about it.'

On another occasion she lost her temper with something and threw a pair of scissors at Lehzen. But although she had outbursts of temper, there was nothing sulky or malicious in Drina's nature. Lehzen often told her she had never looked after such a naughty child. But she had to admit that Drina never told a lie — even if she knew that telling the truth meant that she would be punished. Drina adored Lehzen, although she said later that she had been greatly in awe of her. Her flashes of temper could be blamed partly on her artificial childhood, with no other children to run and shout with. Like the girl in the nursery rhyme, 'When she was good she was very, very good, And when she was bad she was horrid.'

When her lessons were over, Drina played by herself for hours on end, dressing and undressing her collection of 132 small wooden dolls. Dash, her spaniel, also had to put up with being dressed in a scarlet coat and blue trousers. She was surrounded by loving adults and plenty of toys and pets, but as she grew older Drina did miss the company of other children. She had a half-sister, Feodore, but she was twelve years older than herself and left home to marry when Drina was only nine. A little girl called Victoire arrived once a week to play with her 'by appointment'.

All Drina's actions were carefully controlled in this

way. When she was eleven years old, King George IV died and his brother became King William IV. Drina was now heir to the throne, and her life became even more sheltered. She even had to sleep in the same room as her mother right up to the day she became Queen.

Drina did have one continuous source of interesting people. These were her history books, which were the nearest things to adventure stories that she had. But one day she was looking at a book about the kings and queens of England when she came across a page she had never seen before. It had a table of names on it, showing how close to the throne Drina was. Lehzen had decided it was time she began to grow used to the idea. As Drina took it in, her eyes welled with tears. So she would be Queen one day! Turning to her governess she said with complete certainty 'I will be good'.

Few people outside the royal family knew much about Princess Victoria. The Comptroller of the Duchess of Kent's Household, Sir John Conroy, ran everything in the Palace and, though he did arrange various excursions, he was an ambitious, scheming man who hoped for an extremely important position at Court when Victoria became Queen. He thought up lots of ways to emphasize the importance of the Duchess and her daughter, hoping some of it would rub off onto himself. One such idea was that on any visit, their arrival should be heralded by the firing of guns in a royal salute. When this reached the King's ears he was furious and put a stop to it at once.

The King himself foresaw his niece's popularity. He had served in the Royal Navy as a young man, and one day when he was discussing Victoria with a friend, he spoke of her future: 'It will touch every sailor's heart to have a girl queen to fight for. They'll be tattooing her face on their arms, and I'll be bound they'll all think she was christened after Nelson's ship'.

2 In the Wings

Victoria never forgot her seventeenth birthday because one of the visitors to the Palace was her handsome cousin, Albert. Albert was Prince of Saxe-Coburg-Gotha. His father was the eldest brother of Victoria's mother. Albert was just three months younger than Victoria, and, as she wrote in her diary, 'extremely handsome, very clever and intelligent'. She enjoyed singing while he played the piano and sketching with him in the Palace grounds. She had spent so much time alone, that a new companion who shared her tastes was doubly welcome. When the time came for Albert to leave, Victoria cried bitterly, and she lost no time in writing to Uncle Leopold — 'he possesses every quality that could be desired to render me perfectly happy'.

Uncle Leopold, who was now King of the Belgians, and therefore lived in Brussels, sent a good friend to Kensington Palace to be Victoria's advisor. This was Baron Stockmar, whom Victoria soon learnt to trust completely. He was very eccentric and padded about the corridors in a dressing-gown and slippers or old trousers instead of the regulation court breeches, because of the 'English draughts'. But he was honest to the core, and even at such an early age, Victoria had the gift of seeing through appearances to the person inside.

On her eighteenth birthday, the worsening state of King William's health made Victoria sharply aware of the duty that lay before her. Under the British constitution, the heir to the throne attains his or her majority at the age of eighteen, not twenty-one. So whenever King William died, Victoria would take the throne without any interim period of regency.

'I shall strive to become every day less trifling and more fit for what, if Heaven wills, I am some day to be!' was the birthday entry in her diary.

That day was not long in coming. The King died at 2.00 am on June 20th. Victoria was wakened at 6 o'clock and told that the Archbishop of Canterbury and the Lord Chamberlain were waiting to see her. They wanted to see her alone — without even her mother present.

Victoria knew at once why they were there. They both bowed low as the young girl, dressed in a nightdress and dressing-gown with a shawl thrown over it, came into the room. The Lord Chamberlain knelt and kissed her hand and then, still kneeling, told her of the King's death. Victoria's training in self-control had not been in vain, and Lehzen's encouragement of unselfish virtues came to the fore. Her first thoughts were not for herself, but for the widowed Queen, Adelaide. She told the Lord Chamberlain to express 'my feelings of condolence and sorrow' to her. Having given her first royal command with typical dignity, the young Queen joined her mother and Lehzen, who had been waiting in suspense outside the sitting-room door. Only then did she break down and cry.

Victoria took the chance her new status gave her to seize some welcome independence. For a long time she had hated the stifling restrictions put on her by her mother — often under the influence of Sir John Conroy, who had not given up hopes of power. One of the first things Victoria did was to have her bed removed from her mother's room. She also insisted on seeing her ministers and members of her household 'quite ALONE', as she wrote with special emphasis in her diary. Her mother could see her now only 'by appointment'!

When Victoria and her household moved to Buckingham Palace, the Duchess of Kent was given a suite of rooms well away from her daughter while, to her fury, 'dear Lehzen' had a bedroom next door to the Queen's with an adjoining door. The Duchess, whenever she got a chance to see Victoria, bombarded her with complaints: her suite was far too small, she was treated like a complete nobody, she disapproved of Victoria riding through the London streets, her allowance was a pittance (Victoria had increased it to £30,000 a year, but Conroy's 'management' of her affairs had led to enormous debts which she tried to conceal from her daughter).

For the first three years of Queen Victoria's reign, her Prime Minister was Lord Melbourne, whose influence on her became greater even than that of her Uncle Leopold. His cynical view of life, together with his sense of humour provided an ideal contrast to the Queen's strict upbringing. 'It is a source of great amusement to me to collect his 'sayings' ', she wrote. 'English doctors kill you, the French let you die', was one typically cynical gem. One day the Duke of Richmond happened to remark how disgraceful it was that people often came out of prison worse than they went in. 'I am afraid there are many places one comes out of worse than one went in', drawled Melbourne, 'one often comes out worse of a ballroom than one went in'. The Queen roared with laughter.

Lord Melbourne was 58, when he became Victoria's Prime Minister. He had been extremely handsome, and Victoria still found him so, especially — as she confided to her diary — when his hair was ruffled by the wind! She was also attracted by his character, thinking him 'very good' — always the most important quality to her. His influence on her, at a most impressionable time in her life, was immense. When they discussed Christian names, Melbourne said he thought Alice 'beautiful' and Louise 'fastidious'. Was it coincidence that Victoria later chose these names for two of her daughters?

Melbourne boosted the young Queen's self-confidence. He assured her that her lack of height was no drawback. The contrast between her size and the dignity of her bearing only heightened the regal effect. He told her that her nervousness was a sure sign of a 'sensitive temperament', and that people with small 'squeeny' noses 'never did anything!' Although Melbourne's sophistication did much to educate the Queen, he also shielded her from reality. She was genuinely interested in people and wanted to know the facts about her subjects' lives — even the unpleasant ones. But Melbourne told her that all discontent was due to a handful of troublemakers. Victoria had studied Irish history with Lehzen. What, she asked, happened to the 'poor Irish' when they were evicted by their landlords? 'They became *absorbed* somehow or other,' replied Melbourne smoothly, making everyone laugh. 'They ate too much and there was not enough for them and you,' he added. Melbourne always assured Victoria that things were better than they seemed. And this assurance was delivered with so much wit and charm, that the young Queen was only too happy to accept it.

3 Queen and Country

On June 21st, 1837, Victoria was proclaimed Queen from an open window in St. James's Palace. The names Alexandrina Victoria rang out for the last time. At the Queen's wish, she was to be known from now on simply as Victoria. Little Drina had gone for ever.

The new Parliament was opened by Victoria in November. All the leaders of the country were very impressed by her stately bearing and her attractive, musical voice. The final part of her speech referred to her own youth and her reliance on the loyalty of her people. Lord Melbourne, standing beside her, was moved to tears, which was strange, as he had written the words!

The Coronation was fixed for June 28th, 1838, and Melbourne persuaded the Government to spend an enormous amount of money on it. Crimson and gold drapings were ordered for the interior of Westminster Abbey. The court jewellers made the brilliant Imperial State Crown, which is worn today by Queen Elizabeth II when she opens Parliament. It was set with more than 6,000 diamonds, sapphires, emeralds and rubies.

The procession would provide a glittering show for the people, and many of them, leading grim lives, would be only too glad for a glimpse of brightness. In 1838 Britain was becoming 'the workshop of the world' and trade was booming. Many were making fortunes, but many more found themselves on the scrap-heap when new steam-driven engines put them out of a job. There was no public welfare system, and often the only choice left was between the workhouse and starvation.

Only about half of Victoria's subjects could read and write. Small children worked long hours in factories to help their families, and there was little to do in the few hours leisure they did have. In 1838, the whole of industrial Lancashire — including Manchester and Liverpool — had only one public park.

Victoria learned about the seamy side of British life when she read *Oliver Twist* by one of her favourite authors, Charles Dickens. She eagerly persuaded Lord Melbourne to read it, but he was not impressed. He found the details of 'workhouse and coffin-makers and pickpockets' very sordid. He tried to avoid hearing about the plight of the poor in real life, and reading about it in books was not his idea of enjoyment!

As her Coronation day approached, Victoria couldn't help feeling nervous. She was, as yet, naïvely unaware of her effect on people. It was not until much later that she learnt that she could put someone in his place with one withering glance. She did not mind being recognised at the theatres, she told Melbourne, but she feared that the people would grow tired of seeing her. Her Prime Minister found such innocence most amusing.

At 4 o'clock on the morning of her Coronation, the Queen was wakened by the sound of guns in the Park. At

10 o'clock, after dressing in the elaborate Parliament robes of crimson velvet trimmed with ermine, and with a diamond circlet on her head, she stepped into the State coach. Strong sunshine — 'Queen's weather' as it came to be called — flooded the route. The London crowd was swelled by over 400,000 people who had flocked to the capital for the sight of a lifetime.

In the Abbey, before the glittering congregation, the small slim figure of Victoria, at nineteen scarcely more than a child, seemed vulnerable and touching. The supreme moment came when the Archbishop of Canterbury lowered the sparkling crown on to her head. As if planned, a single ray of sunshine shone directly onto it. Then all the peers and peeresses put on their coronets and the trumpets sounded a fanfare.

It was surprising that the Coronation went as well as it did, for there had been no rehearsal. Most of the congregation, intent on watching the young Queen's solemn face, probably did not notice that one of the bishops turned over two pages of the service at once, or that the Archbishop forced the ring onto the wrong finger. Later, Victoria had to bathe her painful finger in iced water to remove the ring. The Archbishop seemed, in fact, totally confused and, at one point, insisted on trying to give Victoria the gold orb when she already had it.

Victoria was encouraged through the gruelling ceremony by Lehzen, who was sitting just above the royal box. The Queen could see her smiling sympathetically down at her. She even managed to give her one of her own sweet smiles in return. Her mother, the Duchess, was not so lucky. She had a seat in the Royal Box but she received no smile from Victoria because she had spent the last few months pestering her with complaints about her place in the procession.

During the Homage, when the peers came, one by one, to give Victoria their oath of fidelity, something happened which gave the crowd some light relief. Old Lord Rolle, who was nearly ninety, tripped over his robes on the steps up to the throne and rolled to the bottom. As he tried to disentangle his legs for a new attempt, the crowd began to cheer. But the Queen's sympathy outweighed her sense of protocol. 'May I not get up and meet him?' she whispered. Then, without waiting for an answer, she went down three of the five steps, held out her hand, and accepted Lord Rolle's tribute there. This simple act of kindness was almost the only natural touch amid all the pageantry. Of course the crowd could not resist seeing the funny side. The fact that it was Lord Rolle who had rolled down the steps was too much for them. Foreigners were assured that it was an ancient tradition that the sovereign should demand a roll from this ancient family as part of its tribute!

At last, after five hours, Queen Victoria drove home in triumph. 'God Save the Queen!' shouted the crowds. But many of those watching did not envy the young girl with the pale, serious face. One such was Thomas Carlyle, the writer. 'Poor little Queen', he wrote 'she is at an age at which a girl can hardly be trusted to choose a bonnet for herself; yet a task is laid upon her from which an archangel might shrink.'

Little did he know. Back at the Palace, Victoria slipped out of her finery, put on an apron and ran upstairs to give her dog, Dash, his bath.

That night, at a banquet in the Palace, Victoria's efforts were rewarded by the person whose praise she had come to value most. Leaning towards his Queen, Lord Melbourne smiled and said, 'You did it beautifully.'

4   Bliss Beyond Belief

Victoria was in no rush to get married. But already her Uncle Leopold was urging her to consider Albert, her German cousin. One thing Victoria was sure of was that she must love her husband — there would be no marriage of convenience.

To Victoria, the most important quality in a person was goodness. But she put beauty almost as high. She enjoyed discussing the handsome figures of her courtiers; she looked for beauty in men as she did in women, animals — and the landscapes she sketched. Victoria could not remember Albert clearly enough to be certain that he would be the right choice and the fact that Lord Melbourne was not enthusiastic about a German match made her hesitate even more. Lord Melbourne was prejudiced against the Germans. He believed that they never washed and were always smoking! But Melbourne knew that if Victoria married an Englishman she would insult a great many people who were not chosen.

Albert, too, was hardly the type to rush into marriage. When he was only four, his beautiful mother had left home leaving him and his brother behind, both with whooping-cough. Although Albert had had a happy childhood with his father and brother Ernest, the absence of a mother had left him ill-at-ease with women and serious to the point of staidness. Any jokes he did play were heavy, well-planned practical jokes — just the opposite of Melbourne's quick puns.

One day in October, 1839, Victoria was out walking, trying to shake off one of her bad headaches. Suddenly she saw a page running towards her with a letter. She wouldn't have to wonder about Albert for much longer. He was arriving that very evening.

Albert had had a dreadful Channel crossing and was as white as a sheet. But as Victoria stood at the top of the stairs at Windsor Castle to greet him, she was completely overwhelmed by his appearance. He had changed. He had grown tall. He was beautiful! His beauty was described in more detail in her diary: 'such beautiful blue eyes, an exquisite nose, and a pretty mouth with delicate moustachios . . . . and a beautiful figure . . .'

On the third day of the visit, Victoria mentioned to Melbourne that seeing Albert again had made her feel quite differently about marriage. 'Wait another week,' advised Melbourne cautiously. But Victoria had thrown caution to the wind. In Albert she was sure she had found the soul mate for whom she had been waiting for so long. If she was *quite* sure, said Melbourne, it was best to marry quickly. There was no point in waiting.

There was only one thing left to do. Victoria must propose to Albert. Of course, Albert could never presume to propose to the Queen of England. That night, Albert, quite unaware of Victoria's thoughts, gave her hand a goodnight squeeze that convinced her that her shy cousin felt the same way about her.

In the morning, Victoria sent for Albert. It was not her way to beat about the bush; she simply told Albert that it would make her 'too happy' if he consented to marry her. Albert needed no persuasion. Taking Victoria in his arms, he kissed her again and again, only breaking off to exclaim in German how wonderful it would be to spend his life with her.

During the days that followed, the cousins grew deeper and deeper in love. They exchanged rings and locks of hair. They danced and went riding. And, most of all, they looked forward to the times they spent alone in the room called the Blue Closet, when they could kiss and ask each other repeatedly, 'Did you expect it — were you surprised?'

Albert's love for Victoria was deep. But he did realize that marrying her would call for a certain amount of courage. In letters home, he assured his family that he would always think of himself as a true German. He knew, too, that he would be homesick at times. His own home was a romantic castle near Coburg, deep in the heart of a forest. In summer he could hear fountains playing through the open windows, and in autumn the stags calling in the distance. He loved the simple country life he lived there; hunting, riding — even gardening. It was a far cry from the pomp and ceremony of his future as Prince Consort. He knew he would always have to take second place to his wife. Back in Germany, preparing for his wedding, Albert was given a taste of this in a letter from his love. She turned down flat his idea of a honeymoon at Windsor lasting longer than two

or three days. 'You forget, my dearest love, that I am the Sovereign and that business can stop and wait for nothing.' Albert did not forget again.

The wedding day — February 10th, 1840, drew near. Victoria was showered with presents, including a new

Scotch terrier, Laddie. When Albert arrived back in England, any doubts caused by the months' separation vanished. Remembering her Coronation, Victoria insisted on a rehearsal of her wedding — and she took special care to try on the ring. Albert had had another dreadful Channel crossing and was pale and nervous. But the Queen was radiantly happy and full of high spirits. She went to bed blissfully aware that it was the last night she would sleep alone.

On her wedding morning, Victoria dressed in a white satin dress and a diamond necklace and earrings. At her throat flashed the sapphire brooch which Albert had given her. She wore, not a crown, but a simple wreath of fresh orange-blossom which she later sketched before it faded. Victoria was almost too excited to notice the crowds as she drove to the Chapel Royal, St James's, in a carriage with her mother. The ceremony passed smoothly, and the Queen was relieved to find she felt much more happy than nervous. A huge wedding breakfast followed. The massive cake was topped by a figure of Britannia, giving her blessing to the royal couple, who were shown as figures dressed in the robes of ancient Romans. Then — very quickly it seemed to Victoria — it was time to set off from the Palace to Windsor Castle for their honeymoon. All along the route the cheers of the people rang in their ears.

How marvellous it was to be alone together at Windsor! They explored the new suite of rooms — running from room to room like children. Three happy days followed. Victoria found that it was 'bliss beyond belief' to wake and find Albert's face on the pillow next to hers. On her return to London she at once sought out her old friend, Lord Melbourne. Never, she told him with shining eyes, had she dreamed that such happiness was in store for her.

5 Storm in the Nursery

With Albert at her side, life took on an exciting new flavour for Victoria. Of course she loved their walks round the garden, playing duets on two pianos and reading aloud to each other. But even the boring business of signing State papers became a delight when Albert helped her with the blotting paper.

Albert did not completely share his wife's happiness. After his father had left to return to Germany, Albert was found by Victoria in the hall weeping bitterly. He rushed past her up to his room. She followed and tried to console him, but he explained that she could not understand his feelings. She had never known her father and her childhood had been miserable compared to his which had now gone for ever!

Albert's homesickness took a long time to fade. Matters were not helped by the Queen's old governess Lehzen — now Baroness Lehzen. She still had enormous influence on Victoria. Too often, it seemed to Albert, when the couple were alone, Lehzen would poke her large beaky nose round the door and call the Queen to some business from which he was shut out. He began to hate her and came to dread the smell of the caraway seeds which she loved to chew. Albert decided not to make too much of

his feelings about Lehzen, but to wait patiently and see if things improved. He couldn't help remembering that she had been almost the only source of happiness in Victoria's lonely childhood.

Soon he was distracted from these problems by the birth of their first child. The baby — a girl — was born just over nine months after their marriage.

'Oh madam, it's a Princess,' the doctor informed the

Queen, in the same tone of voice he used when someone had died.

'Never mind,' said the Queen promptly, 'the next will be a Prince.' She did not seem in the least disappointed, and astonished everyone by the way in which she tucked into the huge meal that she was offered just after the birth.

The baby was christened Victoria Adelaide Mary

Louise, but while she was still a small baby the Queen referred to her simply as 'the Child'. Later she became known as Pussy. 'I'm not Pussy! I'm the Princess Royal!' she once shouted, stamping her feet in much the same way as her mother had done in her own nursery. When she grew older, Pussy was called Vicky.

Queen Victoria did not dislike children, but she did not have much patience with babies while they were only capable of what she called 'that terrible froglike action'. She certainly had no intention of feeding the baby herself, and a wet nurse was hired to breast-feed the baby in her place.

Pussy was scarcely christened when Victoria discovered, to her dismay, that she was going to have another baby. Victoria did not enjoy pregnancies and births. She usually referred to all the details of such things in German, as if this made them seem more delicate. The Queen had been right. Her next child was the Prince of Wales. Albert Edward, known as Bertie, was born on November 8th, 1841. He was a robust, healthy infant. By contrast, little Pussy had become thin and pale and her parents were very worried about her.

In their worry, they had their first serious quarrel. Albert was convinced that Lehzen was at the root of this problem — as of so many others. She was very jealous of her position in caring for the 'nursery darlings'. Albert was sure that Pussy was not being looked after properly, and his hatred of Lehzen brought out a fury in him that was more devilish than was worthy of Victoria's 'Dearest Angel'. He described Lehzen in a letter as 'a crazy, stupid intriguer, obsessed with the lust of power'.

Old Baron Stockmar became a go-between for Victoria and Albert, carrying letters back and forth. Victoria begged Albert not to believe the stupid things she said when she was 'in a passion' — like saying she was sorry she had ever married him. She told Albert she saw Lehzen much less often than he thought. All she wanted was to give her old governess a place in her home in return for all she had done for Victoria in the past.

But Albert was not convinced. At last Victoria agreed that the nursery should be reorganised, and Lehzen must go. Albert made all the arrangements. While Victoria and Albert were in Scotland, Lehzen stayed behind with the children, and began showing others how to do the duties she had carried out for so long. Everything was to carry on as normal, for her mistress's sake. Even her letters were to be pressed in the same way — the Queen could not be expected to read a letter with folds in it.

Lehzen finally left in the autumn of 1842. It seemed as if Victoria has been the better judge of her character. She did not make a scene. Instead she slipped off in the early morning, without even saying goodbye to Victoria in case it would upset her. She went to live with her sister in Germany, where she received a pension from the Queen. Victoria frequently wrote her warm friendly letters and visited her from time to time until she died at the age of eighty six.

To Albert, Lehzen's departure from the Palace was like the sun coming out after a storm. At last his wife was all his own. He described the new Victoria to his brother proudly as 'the most perfect companion a man could wish for'.

6 Candle Ends and Christmas Trees

In 1841, Lord Melbourne's government was defeated and Sir Robert Peel became Prime Minister. Lord Melbourne felt quite happy in leaving Victoria in Albert's hands. He admired the Prince's steady, hardworking character and advised Victoria to rely completely on her husband.

Meanwhile, Albert had shaken off his home sickness and was finding his feet. His German love of order was shocked at the way in which the Royal Household was run. Spurred on by his victory in the nursery, he set about a personal campaign of reforming the whole Court.

There was plenty of room in which his new broom could sweep. Vast amounts of money were squandered in the palace. Thousands of people, who were not entitled to them, had free dinners at Court. Complete strangers used the royal carriages by forging the names of ladies-in-waiting. Mountains of dusters, brushes and mops vanished into thin air every year.

The huge staff of servants seemed to work in complete ignorance of one another. The Department of Woods and Forests cleaned the outside of the windows and the Lord Chamberlain's Department the inside. So they were never completely clean at the same time. Why was the dining-room always icy cold? asked Baron Stockmar, who had never grown used to the British climate. He was told that the fire was laid by the Lord Steward, but had to be lit by the Lord Chamberlain.

Guests at the Palace were amazed at the lack of organisation. Meals were often late. Presents to the Queen stood about unopened in the hall for days. Often, there was no one to show guests back to their rooms in the evening, and they were left to wander about the rabbit warren of corridors. The French foreign minister spent almost an hour looking for his bedroom up and down the stairs at Windsor. At last he found what he thought was the right room and opened the door to find the Queen having her hair brushed by a maid. Another guest gave up the search and settled down for the night on a sofa in the State Gallery. When a housemaid found him there in the morning she assumed he was drunk and fetched a policeman.

Under Albert's direction, the Household was transformed. Even the royal farms began to make a profit. All the parks and gardens were spruced up. No detail was too small for the Prince's eagle eye. All the candles in the main rooms were replaced every day — whether or not they had been used. The staff looked on this as one of their royal perks. Albert soon put a stop to it. Of course the British public took great delight in making jokes about the penny-pinching Prince. He appeared in cartoons, down on his knees poking about in corners for candle ends or counting scrubbing brushes.

Albert also brought order to Victoria. In the security

Albert's love gave her, she blossomed into her favourite role — not Queen, or mother, but Albert's 'Weibchen' (little wife). He was a constant joy to her. And he was brave too. When a madman tried to shoot the Queen when she was driving with Albert, he threw his arms round her and cried 'Don't be alarmed!'

Albert was Victoria's whole life. The only serious arguments they had were about the children. Albert wished Victoria would take more of an interest in them. Even when they were almost grown up, she still relied on him for companionship. It made Victoria very cross when he was busy and suggested that she should spend more time with the children. They were, she snapped, 'no substitute'!

Nothing helped Albert unbend and lose his shyness so much as the rough and tumble of the nursery. In 1843 a second daughter had been born. Princess Alice was called 'Fat Alice' or 'Fatima' by her fond parents. Prince Alfred ('Affie') was born in 1844. The Queen had nine children: Victoria, Albert, Alice, Alfred, Helena, Louise, Arthur, Leopold and Beatrice, the baby, who arrived in 1857. Although she had not wished for quite so many children the fun and games provided by 'our tribe', as she called them, made a happy contrast to her own childhood.

Osborne House, on the Isle of Wight, was especially well-suited to relaxed family life. Albert himself had designed the house. He had aimed for comfort and, although still large and splendid, the house was a far cry from the chilly grandeur of Buckingham Palace. Every room had a V & A entwined over the door — except for

the smoking room. Victoria disapproved of smoking and here the A stood alone.

Victoria could bathe in the sea at Osborne, dressed in a long, tent shaped bathing dress and a large hat. She could have breakfast in the summer house and sketch her children as they pottered about the 'Little Paradise'. Albert brought over a genuine Swiss cottage, section by section and had it set up in the grounds. Here the boys could learn carpentry and gardening and the girls housekeeping and cookery. All the furniture was scaled down to their size and there were two small charcoal ranges with specially-made saucepans. The children invited their parents to teas they had prepared themselves.

Bertie, the Prince of Wales, worried his parents. He was not nearly as clever as his elder sister Vicky, and he seemed to have inherited Albert's serious, rather dull

manner. Albert began to plan his education, and hired a tutor. When Bertie did not seem to be improving at his lessons, the tutor was changed. But it looked as if the trouble lay not with the tutors, but with Bertie. Rumours spread that the Queen thought the Prince of Wales was stupid. At least, she consoled herself, he was honest and good.

The peak of family life came at Christmas. Albert ordered Christmas trees from the forest round his home at Coburg. Victoria was thrilled with this idea, and soon the whole country had followed their lead and Christmas trees stood in thousands of parlours. Albert played blind man's buff with the ladies. He built Victoria a snowman over 3.5 metres high, and he steered the sledge, with Victoria and the children hanging on tight and laughing, out across the snow with its bells jingling. As she watched her handsome husband skating across a

frozen pond or sitting reading by the fire, Victoria counted her blessings. 'Oh! If I could only exactly describe our dear happy life together.'

7 Alone

Victoria thought Albert was working too hard. He got up before dawn in winter and worked at his desk by lamplight. As well as the mountains of paperwork, he began to take some of the Queen's responsibilities off her shoulders. He discussed affairs of State with her ministers and wrote letters which she simply had to copy out. People began to call Victoria 'Queen Albertine'.

The grand climax of Albert's efforts was the Great Exhibition. It was his idea to hold an international festival in Hyde Park. It would be housed in a building specially constructed out of huge glass domes. Albert's romantic streak showed in his choice of name for it — the Crystal Palace. Albert insisted that this should be a practical exhibition — showing the wonders of engineering as well as the beauty of art. He wanted to spread his own belief in the joy of honest labour among as many of the people as possible. He even built two 'ideal' worker's cottages opposite the Crystal Palace.

His grand plans, however, met with problems. At home, the public objected to foreign exhibitors — wouldn't they steal their business? Meanwhile, foreign royalty distrusted Albert's idea of including *all* the people, and most of them stayed away. There were technical problems too. Thousands of birds roosted in the trees under the domes and the noise and the mess were appalling.

The Queen opened the exhibition on Mayday, 1851, and, in honour of the occasion, she wore the famous Koh-i-Noor diamond. She was enchanted with the sights — some more than others. The beautiful display from the French courts and stunning pearls from India appealed to her more than the new American machinery. There was so much to see, that the Queen visited the Crystal Palace almost every day until she left London at the end of July. Despite the initial problems, the exhibition was a resounding success, and Victoria declared the day it closed, October 15th, the 'happiest, proudest day' of her life.

The spirit of international brotherhood shown by the Great Exhibition did not last long. In March, 1854, the Crimean War broke out when Britain, France and Sardinia went to help Turkey resist Russia's attempt at expansion. Although the Russians were stopped, British soldiers suffered terribly because of the appalling conditions. Their old, out-of-touch Generals didn't help matters. The poem, 'The Charge of the Light Brigade' described the most famous example of their bungling. Victoria was horrified at the number of soldiers who died from diseases such as cholera. She presented the famous crusading nurse, Florence Nightingale, with a special gold brooch which read 'Crimea. Blessed are the merciful'.

In March, 1861, a more private sorrow hit the Queen when her mother died. Victoria became ill with grief

and remorse. Although her mother had had her faults, Victoria now missed her and felt deserted. She had been too young to understand when her father died: her mother's death was all the more shocking.

In November of that year, Albert discovered that, while in Ireland with the Army, Bertie had 'disgraced himself' with a woman called Nellie Clifden. Albert loathed this kind of thing. It came at a bad time too. The Queen's outbursts of grief over her mother's death and his own overwork had already worn him out. He was exhausted by lack of sleep and was suffering from aches which he put down to 'rheumatism'. But he felt obliged

to go and see his son when he returned to Cambridgeshire in order to impress on him the gravity of what he had done. Walking about in the cold, damp country lanes, thrashing out the matter, did not help Albert's health. On his return to Windsor, Victoria was startled by his appearance. She could not help remembering how he had once told her that his will to live was much weaker than her own. If he had a serious illness, he said, he would give up at once.

Albert's doctor assured Victoria that there was no cause for concern. He felt that if Victoria was worried, Albert would see it in her eyes and stop trying to fight his illness. Dr Clark's determination that the Prince should not be alarmed, stopped him from being properly treated. Days passed before Victoria realised that Albert's 'chill' was, in fact, the dreaded typhoid fever. Eventually Albert's mind began to wander. He stumbled about the corridors, rattling doorknobs, and asking his doctors to move him from one room to another. At last he sank exhausted into bed in the Blue Room and managed a few last snatches of German to Victoria, who felt as if she was in a nightmare. All the children, apart from Beatrice, the baby, trooped in and kissed his hand. Albert died on December 14th, with Victoria at his side. She kissed his forehead and cried out bitterly 'Oh! My dear Darling!' before she fell to her knees in utter despair. Later, she was led away and her older children tried to comfort her. But everything had gone black. Her whole life had died with Albert and there was no comfort to be found ever again.

Victoria was distraught. Her world was changed overnight. For the four decades that stretched in front of her, she dressed only in widow's black. Albert's memory became an obsession with her. She gave orders that his dressing-gown and fresh clothes should be laid out each evening on his bed and a jug of hot water placed on his wash-stand. The glass from which he had taken his last dose of medicine stood on the same spot on the table for forty years. To make sure that his room could be preserved exactly the same for ever, the Queen had it photographed from all angles. Each night she went to bed clasping Albert's nightshirt; a cast of his hand lay next to her on the pillow, where she could touch it during the night. A whole series of heavy, ornate monuments to Albert were built. Victoria's new mourning writing paper had such wide black borders that the ends of words disappeared into them and were lost for ever — to the exasperation of those who received the letters.

The Court began to fear that the Queen was going mad. There were rumours that she spoke to a bust of Albert and asked his advice on State matters. Victoria suffered from shock for a long time. She had never let herself think about the unthinkable, and now that it had happened, how was she to go on alone? Her children managed to distract her a little — especially Beatrice, with her innocent chatter. She was brought in every morning to play on the Queen's bed.

Other attempts at comfort struck a false note. When a clergyman suggested that the Queen should now look on herself as the bride of Christ, she snapped, 'That is what I call twaddle!'

Victoria retreated more and more into her shell. She refused to open Parliament or attend any public occasion. She finally agreed to be present when Bertie married the beautiful Princess Alexandra in March, 1863, but she sat alone and left before the wedding breakfast. She blamed the Prince of Wales for his father's death. If he had not rushed off to see Bertie he might never had caught the fever. 'I never can or shall look at him without a shudder', she wrote to Vicky.

After the Prince had set off with his bride on their honeymoon, Victoria walked to the huge mausoleum at Frogmore where her beloved Albert was buried. It seemed such a short time since they had set off so happily in their own bridal carriage! After a while Victoria walked back to her suite at Windsor Castle, where she could shut the door on all intruders. She was painfully aware that another door had shut for ever — on the happiest chapter of her life.

8 Life Goes On

The Court and the country grew worried as time passed and the Queen showed no sign of returning to public life. The place where she felt most sheltered from the outside world was Balmoral Castle, in the Scottish Highlands. The interior had been designed by Albert, who had covered every possible surface with tartan. There was tartan wallpaper, tartan curtains — even tartan carpets and chair covers. Any area which had escaped the Prince's 'tartanitis' was smothered in thistle patterns.

Albert had loved Balmoral — not only because the countryside reminded him of his birthplace, but also because of the natural life the family could live there. He went out shooting dressed in a kilt, often accompanied by his favourite gillie, John Brown. It was not surprising that, after Albert's death, Victoria came to rely more and more on the servant her husband had praised so often.

John Brown was a strong-looking man with curly hair and beard. He was very down-to-earth, and the brusqueness of his manner appealed to Queen Victoria. Unlike some of the people at Court, he spoke to Victoria without a trace of the unnatural, fawning behaviour

which she hated and could always detect. Quite the opposite. To the amazement of visitors from London, he addressed the Queen as 'wumman'.

'Hoots then wumman', he was heard to shout at her when he pricked her chin while fixing the strap of her bonnet, 'can ye no hold yer head up?' Victoria felt very safe when Brown was with her. His only fault was his occasional drunkenness. Victoria ignored this or, if it was too obvious to be ignored, put it down to 'bashfulness'. He always seemed to know what the Queen wanted without being asked. After a lifetime of giving orders, his rough kindness must have been very refreshing to Victoria. When she remarked that the cup of tea which Brown had made for her was especially good, he said so it should be — there was a good nip of whisky in it. A maid-of-honour saw Brown with a hamper and asked whether the Queen was having her tea out-of-doors. 'Well, no,' she was told, 'she don't much like tea. We tak oot biscuits and sperruts.'

Victoria became more and more dependent on Brown

and refused to go out riding with any other servant. Brown inspired a lot of dislike and jealousy at Court, but it looked as if the only way of getting the Queen out and about was to bring him South. So, at the end of 1864, Brown was brought down to Osborne. By 1865, he was promoted to 'The Queen's Highland Servant'. Victoria was delighted. 'It is a real comfort', she wrote to her Uncle Leopold, 'for he is devoted to me — so simple, so intelligent, so unlike an ordinary servant.'

The rest of the Court thought Brown was far too unlike an ordinary servant. The Queen favoured him above all other servants — even, at times, above her friends and family. Brown did not like being kept up late — so the smoking-room closed at midnight. On the other hand, he was an early riser. One of Victoria's sons-in-law went out shooting at Osborne one morning, only to find that Brown had been out before him and bagged all the birds. Brown had none of the social graces. The Mayor of Portsmouth once went to ask the Queen to attend a review. As he sat with his private secretary waiting for her official answer, they were both startled by Brown's head coming round the door and barking 'the Queen says saretenly not'.

At least Brown could stand up to the Queen and make her do what she did not feel like doing. This lack of formality with her did, however, lead to many rumours — had she married him in secret?

His unusual, kilted appearance and his Scots accent made him an easy target for jokes. One magazine published a comic account of the Queen opening the Albert Hall; in fact, she had just laid the foundation

stone. The account had apparently been sent in by a Highlander with second sight!

In February, 1866, the Queen opened Parliament for the first time since Albert's death. She looked on this as a real ordeal — 'a show', through which she would be 'dragged in deep mourning, ALONE in State ......'. Instead of the crown, she wore a sombre black cap. She kept a few other public engagements — but they were always a dreadful strain.

Then, in 1868, Benjamin Disraeli became Prime Minister. The Queen was at first distrustful of 'Dizzy' as

he became known by the people. Albert had never liked him — and that counted for almost everything with Victoria. But she had to admit that his speech on the Albert Memorial had been so touching it had made her weep. Disraeli set out to woo the Queen with flattery. 'Everyone likes flattery', Disraeli once said, 'and when you come to royalty you should lay it on with a trowel'. He told Victoria she possessed abilities and judgement 'which few living persons, and probably no living prince, can rival'. Had Disraeli been merely an idle flatterer, Victoria would have seen through him, as she had

through so many others. But he was also very entertaining. He wrote her long, amusing letters — such letters as she had never had before in her life, she exclaimed. His wit and wisdom led her to state that she 'never before knew *everything*'.

Disraeli genuinely enjoyed the Queen's company and was relaxed enough with her to make her relax herself. His political rival Gladstone was, by contrast, a very staid companion. 'Gladstone treats the Queen like a public department; I treat her like a woman', quipped Disraeli.

In December, 1868, Gladstone took Disraeli's place as Prime Minister in a Liberal Government. Victoria had had very high opinions of Gladstone, describing him as 'a *good* man' — her highest compliment. But after Disraeli's sparkling conversation, Gladstone's company was a disappointment. She came to the conclusion that he was pompous and high-minded. He had none of Disraeli's warmth which had broken through the formal relationship and made her feel like an interesting person in her own right.

9 Celebrations

Victoria's life of seclusion continued to give Gladstone what he called the 'blue devils'. But, in 1871, something happened which changed everything. The Prince of Wales, who was now thirty, caught typhoid fever.

The Queen's view of Bertie had mellowed. Although she still felt that he spent far too much time 'gadding about' with unsuitable friends, wasting his life on pleasure, she had also come to appreciate his good qualities and looked forward to the times he spent at home with her. His illness was, for her, an almost unbearable strain. When he recovered from the 'very verge of the grave', Victoria was ecstatic. The shock of his illness even seemed to have improved him. He appreciated small, ordinary pleasures again, like sitting in the garden in the sun.

Gladstone tried to make the most of the Queen's happy mood by suggesting a public celebration: a procession through London, followed by a service of thanksgiving at St Paul's Cathedral. The Queen finally agreed. She even entered into the spirit of celebration and began to make her own suggestions: she would travel in an open carriage; there would be flags in the streets; all the church bells would ring out. The people were more enthusiastic than anyone could have guessed. Victoria's carriage was greeted all along the route by deafening cheers. There was dancing in the streets and the whole nation let its hair down. The Queen's first attempt for so long at 'gadding about' was met with wild enthusiasm.

Victoria was very glad when, in 1874, Gladstone was defeated and a new Government came to power under her old friend Disraeli. Basking in the warmth of Disraeli's flattery, Victoria began to take a keen interest in the country's affairs again. Disraeli called the Queen 'the Faery'. It would be hard to think up a name less suited to the small, plump old woman. But Victoria lapped it up. She used to send Disraeli bunches of primroses, which she had picked herself, in Osborne, and he kept her supplied with long, gossipy letters.

Their friendship also brought more worldly prizes to them both. The Queen wanted to be 'Empress of India'. It was an appropriate title since, during her reign the British Empire — the pink bits on the map — covered nearly a third of the globe, including India. She was called 'the Great White Queen' by the Africans in her colonies and, more romantically, 'Mother of the Nations' by Disraeli. In 1876 Disraeli managed, after a struggle, to pass a bill and Victoria became V.R.I. — Victoria Regina et Imperatrix (Victoria, Queen and Empress). She was so delighted that she gave Disraeli his own title — Earl of Beaconsfield.

In 1881 Disraeli became ill. He insisted on writing to his 'faery' throughout his illness. But when he was asked if he would like her to visit him, he made his last joke: 'No, it is better not. She will only ask me to take a message to Albert.' He died in April and the Queen mourned him more as a good friend than a Prime Minister.

In 1883 John Brown — her 'best and truest friend' — also died. Victoria missed his strong arm to lift her into her pony chair, for she was now suffering badly from rheumatism. She was suffering, too, from Gladstone, whom she found a complete 'humbug'. He complained that she kept him at arm's length 'outside an iron ring'. It was with relief that Victoria saw Gladstone defeated in 1886, and Lord Salisbury take his place as Prime Minister.

Surrounded by an increasing number of grand-children, Victoria viewed her Jubilee year of 1887 in a peaceful, happy mood. Honours flooded in from all ends of the Empire. Some were stranger than others. Her jubilee was celebrated in one part of India by the opening of the 'Queen Victoria Jubilee Burial and Burning Ground'. At home, Jubilee medals and coins were struck.

On June 21st, the Queen drove through wildly cheering crowds to the Golden Jubilee Service in Westminster Abbey. She delighted the people by travelling in an open carriage drawn by six horses, and wearing a bonnet decorated with diamonds and lace. That night she was kept awake by the roar of the people shouting and laughing in the streets below. Next day, there was a huge party in Hyde Park, at which 30,000 schoolchildren were presented with a bun, milk and a Jubilee mug. When one little girl saw a huge balloon rising from the grass she cried: 'Look! There's Queen Victoria going up to Heaven!' To children, it seemed as if Victoria had reigned for ever. Her Jubilee was a

brilliant success and the Queen was overwhelmed by the love shown to her by millions of her subjects.

In 1892 the 'really wicked' Gladstone came back to power. The Queen had never been able to hide her feelings and she even stopped trying. One hot July day, at the wedding of one of her grandsons, Gladstone, who was not well, sought refuge from the heat in the Queen's marquee. 'Does he think,' snapped Victoria in horror, 'that this is a public tent?' What a contrast to her earlier treatment of Disraeli, whom, despite the normal conventions, she had begged to sit down in her presence. It pleased Victoria greatly when Gladstone retired in 1894 because of his bad health.

Victoria's Diamond Jubilee in 1897 was greeted with even more enthusiasm than her Golden one. This time the short service of thanks was held in front of St Paul's, as the Queen's rheumatism, by now crippling, stopped her from climbing the stairs. But even with her failing eyesight, she could see that the cheering faces in the crowd were 'filled with joy', and they helped her to forget her pain.

Her Diamond Jubilee day was put away with all the other memories — happy and sad — that Victoria had gathered through her long life. Now, at nearly eighty, her bad eyesight was causing problems for her staff. She insisted on being kept in touch about even trivial matters. Eventually, papers had to be read out to her, though her mind remained as sharp as ever and her hold on her Household just as tight.

Victoria's last years were brightened by her forty-odd grandchildren, who called her 'Gangan', and whose easy